Allergies

© Aladdin Books 1990

*First published in
the United States in 1990 by*
Franklin Watts Ltd
387 Park Avenue South
New York NY 10016

Design: David West Children's Book Design
Editor: Claire Llewellyn
Picture Research: Cecilia Weston-Baker
Illustrator: Ian Moores

Printed in Belgium

The publishers would like to acknowledge that the photographs reproduced within this book have been posed by models or have been obtained from photographic agencies.

Library of Congress Cataloging-in-Publication Data

White, T., MD.
    Living with allergies by T. White, MD
        p cm – (Living with)
    Includes bibliographical references.
    Summary: Surveys the many aspects of allergies, including their treatments and dangers, and identifies some famous people who live with allergies.
    ISBN 0-531-10857-0
    1. Allergy--Juvenile literature. [1. Allergy.] I. Title.
RC584.W48 1990
362.1'9697--dc20   89-29454   CIP AC

CONTENTS

WHAT ARE ALLERGIES?   4

WHAT CAN GO WRONG?   8

TESTS AND TREATMENTS   18

LIVING WITH ALLERGIES   26

GLOSSARY   31

INDEX   32

Living with

Allergies

Dr. T. White

FRANKLIN WATTS

London : New York : Toronto : Sydney

WHAT ARE ALLERGIES?

Every day we come into contact with things that may harm us. These may be things that we eat or drink, chemicals in the world around us, molds or viruses. Our bodies have an elaborate defense system which protects us from these dangers. It is called our immune system, and all the time it is fighting battles against the things which may harm us. If our immune system loses a battle, we may fall ill, but this is rare, and most of us are healthy most of the time.

The immune system is not a separate structural system like the nervous system. Rather, it is the body's normal response to infection. It involves a number of organs in the body and the substances that they make. Together, these act in a coordinated and systematic way to protect the body from harmful substances. In some people, the immune system reacts at the wrong time or against the wrong thing. This unwanted reaction is called an allergy.

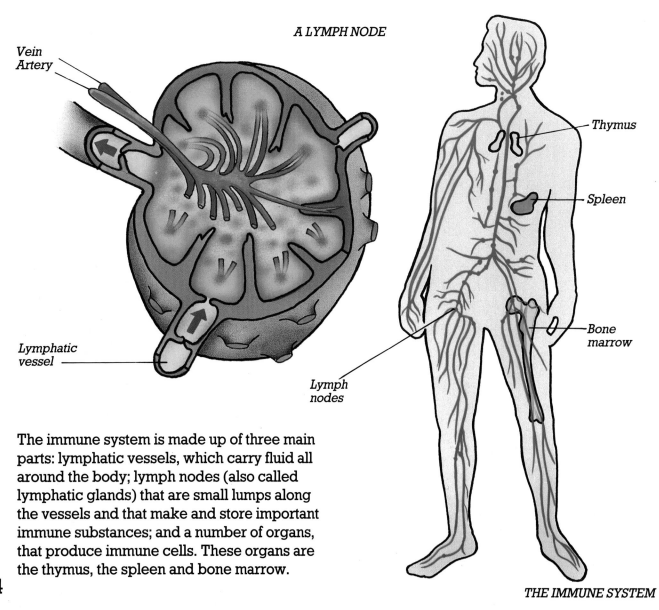

A LYMPH NODE

Vein
Artery

Lymphatic vessel

Thymus

Spleen

Bone marrow

Lymph nodes

The immune system is made up of three main parts: lymphatic vessels, which carry fluid all around the body; lymph nodes (also called lymphatic glands) that are small lumps along the vessels and that make and store important immune substances; and a number of organs, that produce immune cells. These organs are the thymus, the spleen and bone marrow.

4

THE IMMUNE SYSTEM

Lymph node

Vein

Artery

Blood capillaries

Small lymphatic vessels

Small lymphatic vessels are closely linked to blood capillaries. Immune cells can then enter the blood quickly to fight infection.

The immune system

When harmful things enter our body, special cells, called immune cells, fight against them. Large numbers of immune cells are found in the bloodstream, in all the tissues of the body and in the lymph nodes. When immune cells are faced with a threat, they respond rapidly, multiplying to fight the danger and stop it from spreading. This is why the lymph nodes in the neck swell up quickly when you have an infection like a sore throat.

There are several different kinds of immune cell and each kind has its own special name and a special job to do. The most important immune cells are the macrophages, which engulf, or eat up, harmful things that enter the body. Lymphocytes and mast cells are two other kinds of immune cells which have particular jobs. They are explained in the following pages.

This picture shows two macrophages in the lung. The round one (on top) is the usual shape. The flat one (below) is about to eat up the small round particle of dust (bottom left).

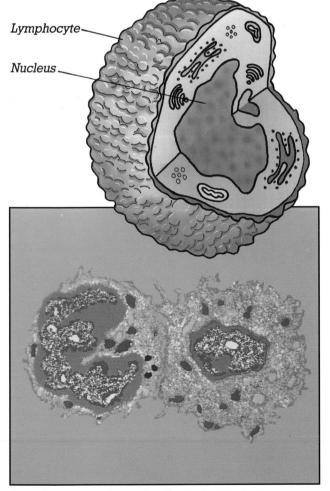

Lymphocyte

Nucleus

Lymphocytes make antibodies to fight infection.

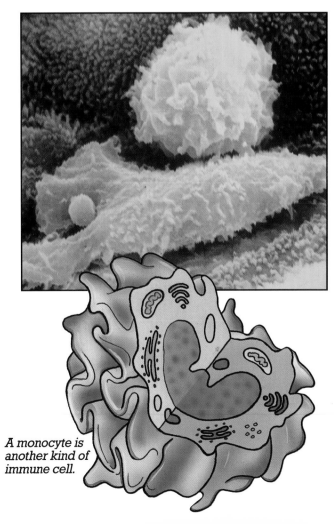

A monocyte is another kind of immune cell.

5

The immune response

Lymphocytes are one kind of immune cell. They make antibodies to fight against antigens. Antigens are substances that enter the body and may be harmful. Each antibody has a special shape and will fit only one kind of antigen, like a key in a lock. Together, the antibody and antigen make up an immune complex. Macrophages destroy all the immune complexes, which then leave the body.

Antibodies are made of proteins called immunoglobulins. There are four types of immunoglobulins: IgA (Immunoglobulin A) protects the lungs and gut; IgG and IgM are important antibodies in the blood; IgE is active in a sudden "allergic" response, so is found in the skin for quick action. When a specific antibody has been made, "memory lymphocytes" remember its formula, so that if the same antigen threatens in the future, an even quicker response can be organized.

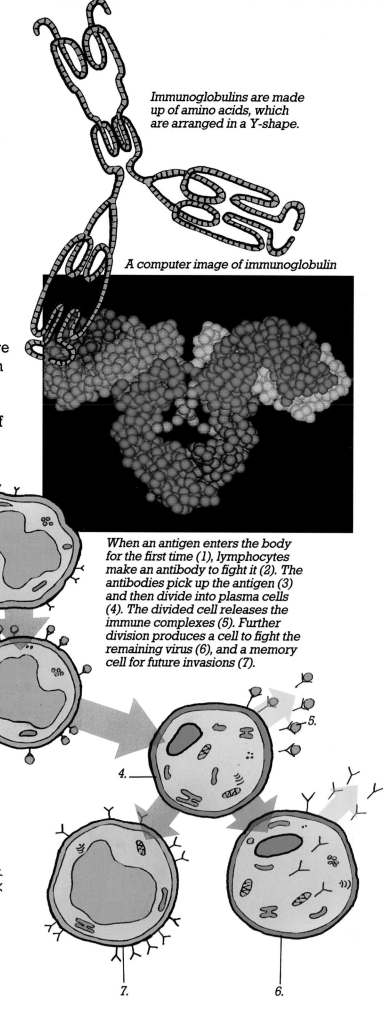

Immunoglobulins are made up of amino acids, which are arranged in a Y-shape.

A computer image of immunoglobulin

When an antigen enters the body for the first time (1), lymphocytes make an antibody to fight it (2). The antibodies pick up the antigen (3) and then divide into plasma cells (4). The divided cell releases the immune complexes (5). Further division produces a cell to fight the remaining virus (6), and a memory cell for future invasions (7).

1.
2.
3.
4.
5.
6.
7.

The allergic response

Sometimes the immune system gets it wrong and fights against substances that are harmless. These substances are called allergens, but the body reacts to them as though they were antigens. This reaction only happens in certain people, and only when the body has already been exposed to the allergen before. We do not know why. IgE antibodies are important in cases of allergy. They attach themselves to cells near the skin, called mast cells. When mast cells are activated by an allergen, they break up and release chemicals, such as histamine, that cause inflammation.

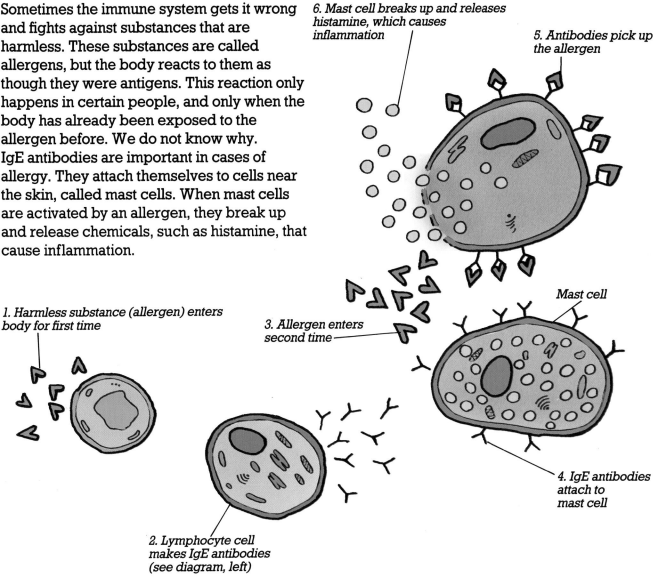

6. Mast cell breaks up and releases histamine, which causes inflammation

5. Antibodies pick up the allergen

Mast cell

1. Harmless substance (allergen) enters body for first time

3. Allergen enters second time

4. IgE antibodies attach to mast cell

2. Lymphocyte cell makes IgE antibodies (see diagram, left)

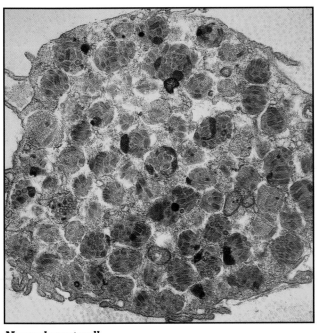

Normal mast cell

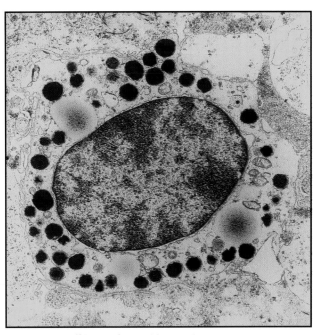

This mast cell has released histamine.

7

WHAT CAN GO WRONG?

Allergy produces two main types of disease. The first type is called atopy and is a tendency to have unusually strong reactions to common allergens like pollen, molds, spores and house dust mites. The second type of disease caused by allergy is called immune complex disease. When an antigen (or an allergen) and its antibody have joined together, they are called the immune complex. They are usually destroyed by macrophages and eliminated from the body. Sometimes, however, this does not happen and they remain in different parts of the body where they cause inflammation and damage, as in the case of rheumatoid arthritis and celiac disease. In other cases, because antigens are proteins, the body may confuse them with its own proteins and make antibodies to fight against them. In effect, the body is fighting itself. The diseases this causes are known as auto-immune disorders and include pernicious anemia.

Hay fever

Hay fever is not a fever at all; it is an allergic reaction to the pollen which is carried on the wind. The reaction occurs in the nose and eyes where pollen, the allergen, reacts with IgE and makes the mast cells break down and release histamine. The symptoms of hay fever are itching, watering eyes, sneezing, congestion and a runny nose. Some people get hay fever in the spring when trees release their pollen, but most hay fever is caused by grass pollens. There is most grass pollen in the air from May to July, and the months of early summer can be a misery for sufferers.

Sneezing is one of the symptoms of hay fever.

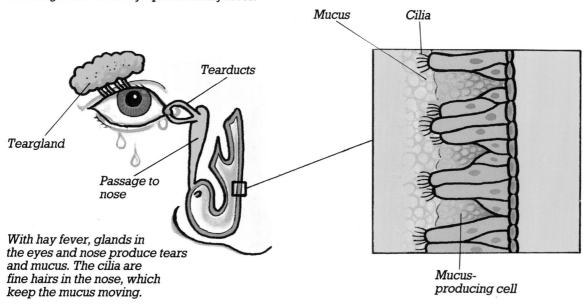

Tearducts

Teargland

Passage to nose

Mucus

Cilia

Mucus-producing cell

With hay fever, glands in the eyes and nose produce tears and mucus. The cilia are fine hairs in the nose, which keep the mucus moving.

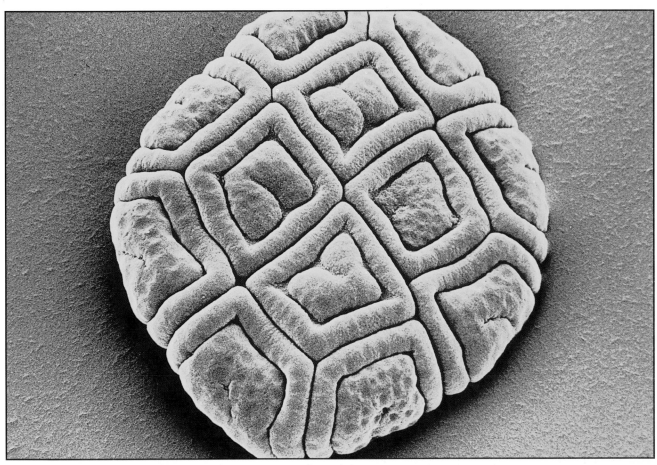

A microscopic view of a pollen grain from mimosa, a flowering tree.

A pollen grain from the flower of chickweed.

9

Asthma

The word "asthma" comes from the Greek word for "panting" or "labored breathing." Approximately one person in ten suffers from asthma to some extent. Asthma causes bouts of wheezing, coughing and shortness of breath and these can be mild, moderate or very severe. Doctors now know that most asthma cases are caused by allergy. The allergy is often to pollen, mold, spores, the tiny mite which is found in house dust or to animal fur. Many asthma sufferers are children. They often improve as they get older, but the tendency to wheeze never leaves them completely. Although the allergen which causes the reaction may be the same as in hay fever, the reaction in asthma is different, and occurs in a different part of the body. If allergens are not removed as air passes through the nose and mouth, some of them may reach the lungs, and it is here that the reaction which causes asthma takes place.

Animal fur can cause asthma.

The common house dust mite causes different allergic reactions.

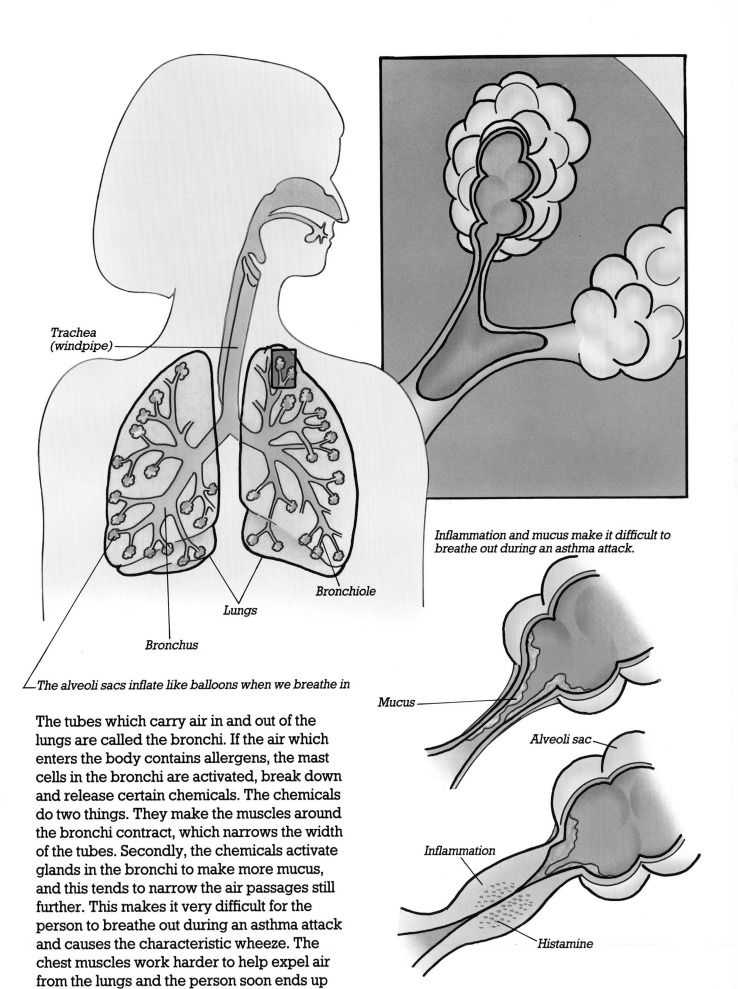

Trachea
(windpipe)

Lungs

Bronchus

Bronchiole

The alveoli sacs inflate like balloons when we breathe in

Inflammation and mucus make it difficult to breathe out during an asthma attack.

Mucus

Alveoli sac

Inflammation

Histamine

The tubes which carry air in and out of the lungs are called the bronchi. If the air which enters the body contains allergens, the mast cells in the bronchi are activated, break down and release certain chemicals. The chemicals do two things. They make the muscles around the bronchi contract, which narrows the width of the tubes. Secondly, the chemicals activate glands in the bronchi to make more mucus, and this tends to narrow the air passages still further. This makes it very difficult for the person to breathe out during an asthma attack and causes the characteristic wheeze. The chest muscles work harder to help expel air from the lungs and the person soon ends up feeling exhausted.

11

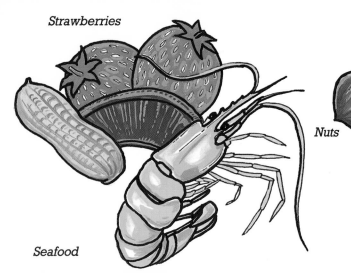

Strawberries

Nuts

Seafood

Hives

Some people are allergic to the proteins in certain foods, especially in nuts, strawberries and seafoods. Sometimes the allergic reaction may only involve IgA (see page 6) and result in swelling lips, a tingling mouth, vomiting and diarrhea. More often, it also involves IgE in the skin tissues. The reaction with the allergen releases histamine in the tissues both in and under the skin. The histamine causes a fairly common condition that doctors call hives. Hives is very unpleasant and produces a characteristic skin eruption, with red patches and blisters that are intensely itchy. This rash can last for anything from a minute up to a week. Asthma, a runny nose and eczema may also result. It is not only foods which can cause this reaction; many viruses (like those that cause coughs and colds), drugs, certain plants, insect bites and intense hot or cold are also known to cause hives in some people. In many cases, the cause of the reaction is never known, which makes repeated attacks difficult to control.

Hives rash

Bee or wasp stings

A few people are so sensitive to particular allergens that a very dangerous reaction can take place called anaphylactic shock. This can sometimes result in sudden death, after a relatively harmless incident like a bee or wasp sting. In anaphylactic shock, the allergic reaction causes such a massive release of histamine and other chemicals that the body's defenses are overwhelmed. Blood vessels widen all over the body, and blood pressure drops so low that the brain and other essential organs cannot work properly. The patient will die unless expert medical care is available at once. Fortunately, this is a very rare reaction and for most of us insect stings are just a painful nuisance. People who know they are allergic to stings should always carry anti-histamine tablets with them (see page 19) in order to counteract such symptoms.

Some people have an extreme allergy to bee or wasp stings – they can prove fatal.

Celiac disease

Celiac disease is just one of the conditions caused by immune complexes. These are the antigen-antibody units explained on page 6. The disease is caused by a reaction to gluten, which is found in wheat flour. Gluten is present in many of the foods we eat: bread, cookies, cakes etc. In celiac disease, antibodies against gluten make immune complexes with the gluten and are deposited in the wall of the first part of the small intestine where gluten, as well as other foods, is usually absorbed. The wall of the intestine is made up of fine folds, called villi, which are damaged by the immune complexes. This interferes with the absorption of all foods and results in diarrhea, weight loss and weakness. Good health returns only when gluten is completely removed from the diet for life. It can never be reintroduced.

Celiac disease is often identified soon after a baby starts on solid food.

Villi

Blood capillaries

Lymph vessel

Villi are fine folds in the wall of the small intestine. They are essential for the absorption of many foods. In celiac disease, villi are damaged, food is not absorbed properly and the patient weakens.

Foods and additives

Much of the food we eat today is processed in some way. Chemicals and other additives are used to keep food fresh on its journey from the producer to the stores, or to improve its appearance or taste. Unfortunately, some people react to the chemicals or additives used in processing. For example, some toddlers become irritable or overactive if they have one of the red or orange colored drinks that contain tartrazine, a dye. Reactions to specific foods are not true allergies, but instead are chemical reactions. That is why the term "food intolerance" is more accurate than food allergy.

Atopic eczema

Eczema is characterized by a rash, with itchy, scaly red patches on the face, neck, elbows and knees. Eczema is quite common in young children and doctors believe it is caused by an allergic reaction (which is why it is called atopic eczema). Certain evidence supports the doctors' view.

* There is often a history of allergies in the family.
* The child often develops asthma or hay fever in later life.
* There may be a known allergen, which could be a food. The foods that often cause a reaction are eggs and milk, particularly cow's milk.

Atopic eczema is different from adult eczema, where an allergy is unlikely to be the cause.

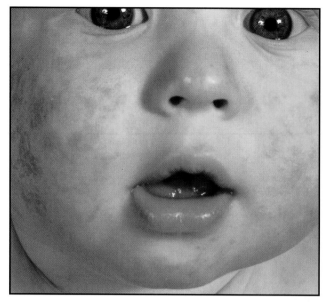

Atopic eczema is a problem for many children.

Cosmetics and chemicals

Some of the chemicals that are used in cosmetics, around the home or in industry, can cause a skin reaction. These are usually chemical reactions, but true allergies can occur. In these cases, the allergens are materials which are harmless to most people, but cause symptoms in sensitive skin. The position and shape of the rash is often a clue to the cause. For example, allergy to nickel in stainless steel in a watch strap would produce a rash around the wrist in the shape of the strap.

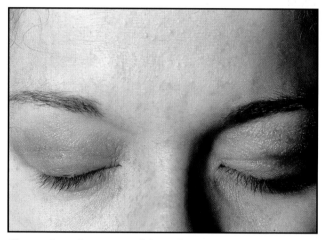

Cosmetics often cause skin rashes.

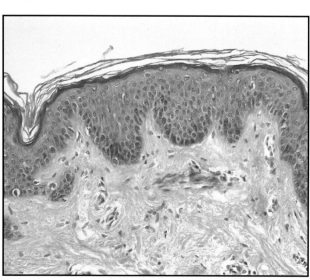

A section of normal skin which shows the surface to be smooth and white.

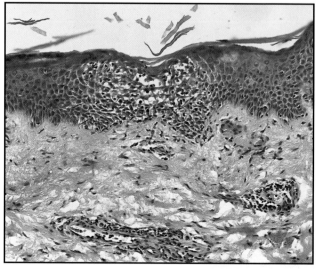

A section of skin in allergic response. Excess blood in the capillaries gives the surface its darker color.

Histamine in nature

The hairs on the leaves and stems of certain plants contain histamine. When touched, the hairs inject small amounts of histamine under the skin, causing a reaction identical to hives wherever the nettle was touched.

The trailing tentacles of jellyfish also contain histamine. A jellyfish sting can be very unpleasant because such a large amount of histamine is injected. Large jellyfish, like the Portuguese man-of-war, can even kill unwary swimmers.

Under the microscope – the stinging nettle

Histamine in jellyfish causes nasty stings.

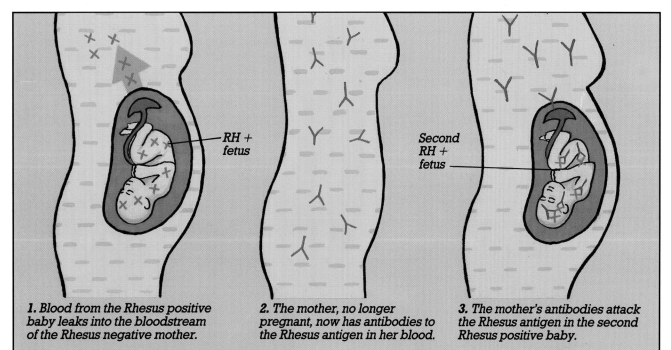

1. Blood from the Rhesus positive baby leaks into the bloodstream of the Rhesus negative mother.

2. The mother, no longer pregnant, now has antibodies to the Rhesus antigen in her blood.

3. The mother's antibodies attack the Rhesus antigen in the second Rhesus positive baby.

Rhesus immunization

Blood is classified in several ways, including the ABO grouping and the Rhesus types. 85 percent of people have the Rhesus antigen in their blood and are known as Rhesus positive. The other 15 percent do not have this factor, and are known as Rhesus negative.

If Rhesus negative people come into contact with the Rhesus antigen, they may make antibodies to fight against it. This is important in pregnancy. Blood types are inherited, so a Rhesus positive father and Rhesus negative mother could have a Rhesus positive baby. The mother may make antibodies against her baby's blood. This will not harm the first baby, but it could damage a second Rhesus positive baby.

Mistaken identity

Normally the body learns at a very early stage to recognize and ignore proteins which belong to itself. However, antigens are proteins too, and occasionally the body may confuse these proteins with its own, and end up making antibodies against itself. This causes auto-immune diseases. Here are examples of four such diseases:

Systematic lupus erythematosus: in lupus, high levels of many types of antibodies are produced and attack a variety of antigens in the body. Damage to the kidneys, liver and nervous system can result.

Pernicious anemia: in this disease, antibodies to certain cells in the stomach prevent the body absorbing vitamin B12. This vitamin is important for healthy red blood cells, and the lack of it causes anemia. The disease is easily treated by occasional injections of vitamin B12 which bypass the stomach.

Rheumatoid arthritis: people who suffer from this disease have an antibody against IgG immunoglobulin in their blood. This may cause the damage to joints which occurs with this disease.

Rheumatic fever: in this disease, the body makes antibodies against a germ called streptococcus. Unfortunately, the valves in the heart have such a similar chemical structure to the toxin that the antibody, unable to distinguish between the two, damages the heart as well as the toxin.

Antibodies

Antigen

Nucleus

LUPUS: antibodies start to attack the nucleus in the body's cells. The nucleus is vital; it controls the cell's activity.

Antibodies attack the invading germ

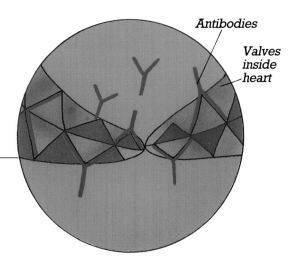

Antibodies

Valves inside heart

RHEUMATIC FEVER: inside the heart, the valves have a similar structure to a germ called streptococcus. The antibody to the germ also attacks the valves. It is not capable of distinguishing between the two.

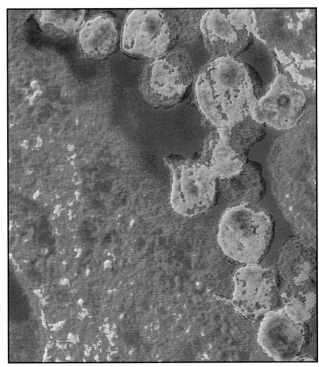

Placenta

Antibodies

Umbilical cord

As a baby develops in the womb, it is protected by the mother's immune system. Antibodies pass freely through the placenta and the umbilical cord. A breastfed baby continues to receive immunity through its mother's milk.

The HIV virus (which causes AIDS) shows up as orange.

Immune deficiencies

So far, we have discussed what can go wrong with a complete immune system. But some people do not have a complete immune system. Doctors call these abnormal systems "immune deficiency disorders." These disorders are not common, but there is a lot of interest in them because of what they can teach doctors about how the immune system works. This has become especially important since the discovery in 1981 of AIDS (Acquired Immune Deficiency Syndrome). Different kinds of disorders are listed below.

Some babies are born with deficient immune systems for various reasons. They may be unable to make enough immunoglobulins of one sort or another, there may be a shortage of immune cells in the body, or the immune cells may not work properly. Sometimes, as in the case of cystic fibrosis, the skin does not act as a good barrier to infections. Germs are able to enter the body more easily, and so children may often get seriously ill.

Some diseases of the immune system, like leukemia (a cancer of the blood cells) or AIDS, will weaken the body's defenses against other infections.

A poor diet which is low in protein increases the risk of infection. In some Third World countries, infections which are not very serious in our country, like measles, can be major killers.

Drugs can also reduce the body's resistance to disease, particularly drugs like steroids, which interfere with the activity of immune cells and may reduce the number of these cells in the body. Sometimes the immune system has to be "damped down" with drugs deliberately. This is done to prevent the rejection by the body of a transplanted kidney, liver or heart.

As people grow older, their immune system works less efficiently. It is well known that people at the two extremes of life – newborn babies and the very elderly – have a low resistance to disease, and therefore are particularly likely to develop infections.

TESTS AND TREATMENTS

In order to diagnose an allergy, a doctor's first step will be to ask for the patient's "case history," in other words, a clear account of the symptoms and the circumstances in which they occurred. Sometimes the history alone will give the answer. For example, if a person comes out in a rash within minutes of eating Brazil nuts, and this rash recurs each time the same type of nut is eaten, then the rash can only be due to the nuts, and the only treatment is to give up eating them!

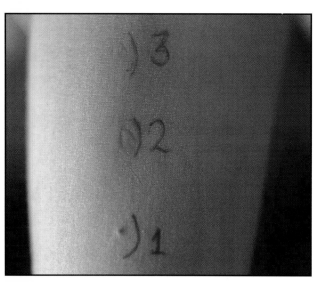
Suspected allergens are pricked into the skin.

A whole range of foods may be eliminated.

After the history, the doctor's next step is a physical examination of the patient. If there is a rash, the doctor will make a note of where it is and what it looks like. Asthma may be diagnosed by listening for a wheeze in the chest, or by measuring the amount of air the patient is able to breathe in and out. The most difficult part of the diagnosis is usually discovering which of the many different kinds of allergen is causing the problem, and special tests are often used for this.

Finding the allergen

There are three kinds of tests which may identify an allergen.

Skin tests: small amounts of suspected allergens are pricked into the skin. A reaction like a mild rash may show that the patient is sensitive to that allergen. However, people who suffer from allergies tend to react to many different substances!

Blood tests: the most useful tests are those that look for antibodies to a particular allergen. If a specific antibody is found in the blood, then it proves that a reaction to that allergen has occurred at some time in the past. This test is useful in detecting Rhesus disease.

Food elimination: an allergy to a particular food is very difficult to detect. Suspected allergens are removed from the diet to see if the patient's health improves. If it improves without the allergen, and then worsens when it is reintroduced, the test is positive. If a large number of foods are suspected, the patient follows an elimination diet, eating nothing except mineral water, lamb and pears (none of which usually causes a reaction). Other foods are introduced one by one to see if a reaction takes place. This test is only done when serious food allergy is suspected.

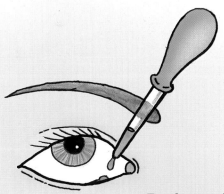

Histamine

Mast cell

Immune
complex

Steroids
prevent the immune complex
from attaching itself to the mast cell.

Mast cell

Cromoglycate stops
the mast cell breaking
up and releasing histamine.

Drugs for allergies

It is often impossible to identify, or perhaps avoid contact with, allergens. Doctors may then use drugs to control the symptoms. Drugs may act at any stage in the allergic reaction. Some drugs act at the beginning of the allergic reaction by preventing the immune complex (allergen-antibody unit) from attaching itself to mast cells. The patient has to take large doses of steroids which may give troublesome side effects. This approach is only used in serious cases. However, smaller, safer doses of steroids can be given by an inhaler, in eye or nose drops or in sprays – and these are used widely to control asthma and hay fever. Other drugs, such as cromoglycate, act later in the allergic reaction, after the immune complexes have attached themselves to the mast cells. These drugs stabilize the mast cells and stop them breaking down and releasing histamine. This is useful for hay fever and asthma. Some drugs act at the last stage of the allergic reaction and counteract the effects of histamine. They are called anti-histamines and are useful in the treatment of hay fever and hives.

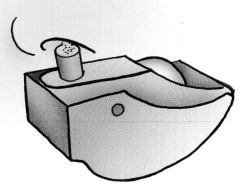

Eye drops and nose sprays are
two common and safe ways of
taking anti-histamine drugs.

There are several ways of taking drugs
for allergies: this machine is called a
compression unit.

Treating hay fever without drugs

If you suffer from hay fever, you should try to reduce your exposure to pollens. It is a good idea to listen for the pollen count at the end of weather forecasts. When the count is high, it is wise to shut the windows and stay indoors. Air conditioning also helps because the filtration removes most of the pollen grains from the air. If you do go outside, avoid areas where grass has been cut recently, or where hay has been harvested. It is best to go out in the early morning or in the evening. In addition, you may find that dark glasses help to protect sore, sensitive eyes. In the United States, doctors have carried out experiments using filtration helmets, that remove pollen from the air before it is inhaled. They are quite successful, but few people are so badly affected by hay fever that they are willing to look like an astronaut!

Dark glasses help to protect light-sensitive, itchy eyes from the sun's rays.

Antibodies attack the allergen before it activates the immune cells.

Small amounts of allergen are injected.

Desensitization

If small doses of an allergen are injected into the body repeatedly, the allergic response can sometimes be "un-learned." What happens is that the small amounts of allergen are intercepted by antibodies before they reach the immune cells. After a course of injections, the immune system learns to tolerate the allergen. However, there are drawbacks to desensitization treatment. Firstly, the treatment does not always work. Secondly, the patient may suffer from rashes or other reactions during the course of the treatment, particularly if the doses of allergen are increased too quickly. Thirdly, no one likes repeated injections. In fact, these injections can be hazardous to very sensitive people, so the treatment is not often used nowadays, especially now that drug treatment is much safer and more effective. Desensitization is most effective in hay fever. It has also been used to treat people who have severe reactions to bee and wasp stings. However, it fails to work with asthma or house dust mite allergy.

Meteorology

During early summer, weather forecasters calculate the pollen count on a daily basis. They do this by measuring the number of pollen grains that are caught in a filter when air is passed through it. The more grains there are in the filter, the more pollen there is in the air. The pollen count is published daily in newspapers, and is announced during the weather forecasts on radio and television. It gives an important warning to sufferers for two reasons. If the count is high, they may choose to stay indoors and reduce their exposure to pollen. Secondly, many of the drugs which are used in the treatment of hay fever need to be taken early in the attack to be most effective. The pollen count is useful to hay fever sufferers, therefore, in helping them to time treatment more accurately. The count is highest in hot, dry weather, particularly if there is also a breeze to stir more of it into the air and carry it farther. The count is lowest in wet weather, when the dampness keeps pollen on the ground.

Hay fever sufferers should avoid grassy areas in early summer.

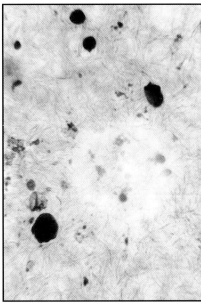

Pollen grains are caught in the filter.

Taking the pollen count.

21

Treatment for asthma

People who suffer from asthma are called asthmatics, and most of them need treatment with drugs. Many of the drugs are fine powders that asthmatics breathe in from a device called an inhaler. Inhaler treatment is very safe and very effective. The drug goes straight into the lungs and works very quickly, so the patient only needs small doses. This prevents the drugs from upsetting the workings of other parts of the body. The drugs which are used most commonly are "bronchodilators." These relax the muscles around the bronchi and open up the airways. Steroids may also be inhaled, as these are the only drugs that reduce the amount of mucus inside the bronchi. Other drugs, like cromoglycate and theophyllines, can also help. Drugs may be taken in one of three ways: during an asthma attack itself; regularly, to prevent attacks; both regularly *and* during an attack.

Using an inhaler to treat asthma

A SECTION OF THE BRONCHUS

Drugs

When drugs like bronchodilators are inhaled, they reach the bronchus quickly, relax the muscles around the bronchus and open the airways.

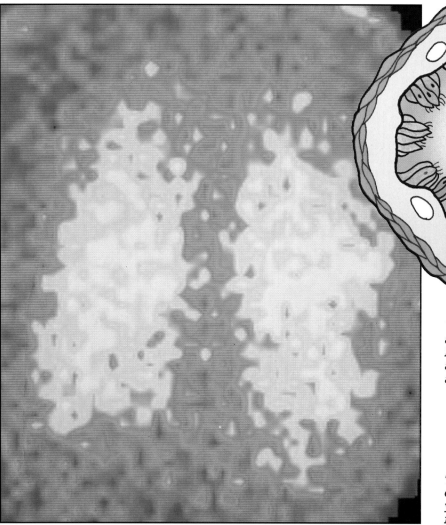

This camera scan shows the lungs of an asthmatic person. The green, yellow and white coloring represents poor ventilation.

A new approach to asthma

Careful drug treatment is the best way to control asthma, and most sufferers now take drugs regularly to prevent attacks. However, there are other, more general ways that asthmatics and their families can help their condition. Try to keep the house as dust free as possible, by regular cleaning. It may be wise to have no animals in the house. In addition, asthmatics are encouraged to exercise, particularly by swimming as it seems less likely to cause wheezing. If any sport does cause wheezing, this can usually be avoided by inhaling a dose of the prescribed drug before starting. The old-fashioned approach of treating asthmatics as delicate, and sending them to special schools, is no longer recommended. With proper care, most asthmatics lead full and active lives. Indeed, many top sports personalities suffer from asthma.

Plenty of fresh air and exercise help asthmatics to maintain good health and fitness.

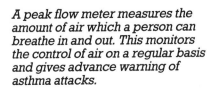

A peak flow meter measures the amount of air which a person can breathe in and out. This monitors the control of air on a regular basis and gives advance warning of asthma attacks.

23

Celiac disease

Doctors are able to diagnose celiac disease by taking a biopsy from the small intestine. A biopsy is a small sample of tissue which doctors take from the body by means of a long flexible tube. The tube goes in the mouth, down into the stomach, and then gently pulls a little tissue from the wall of the intestine. Doctors examine this tissue under a microscope. The appearance of the biopsy tells the doctor whether the patient has celiac disease or not, because diseased tissue looks very different from healthy tissue. The main symptoms of celiac disease are weakness, diarrhea and weight loss. They all quickly improve when the patient stops eating gluten. This means cutting out foods which contain wheat flour. Patients must follow this new diet for the rest of their lives.

Small intestine

Liver

Stomach

Biopsy forceps control

Eye piece

Long flexible tube

Biopsy forceps in the endoscope can snip out a sample for analysis.

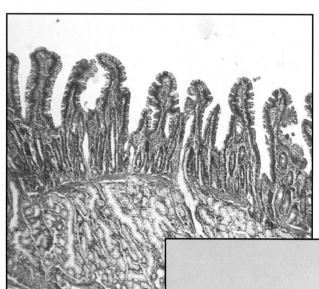

Above:
A biopsy of healthy tissue from the wall of the small intestine shows the villi clearly.

Right:
A biospy of diseased tissue, the result of celiac disease, shows damaged villi which can no longer absorb foods properly.

Rhesus disease and pregnancy

All pregnant women have a blood test to discover whether they are Rhesus positive or negative. Second-time mothers who are negative have another blood test to discover whether they have antibodies against the Rhesus antigen. If antibodies are found, it proves that a reaction to the Rhesus antigen took place with the first baby, whose blood must have leaked into her bloodstream. Doctors then watch the second baby carefully for any problems. This state of affairs is now rare because Rhesus negative mothers are given an injection of anti-D after the birth of their first child. Anti-D is an antibody against the Rhesus antigen which "mops up" any blood from the new baby and prevents its reaching the mother's immune system.

Problems with a second Rhesus positive baby rarely occur today.

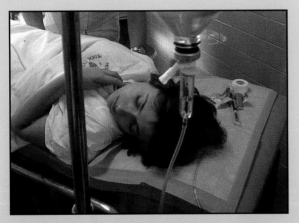

Immunosuppressive drugs given by injection.

Immunosuppressive drugs

Sometimes the whole immune system has to be "damped down" with drugs called immunosuppressive drugs. This form of treatment is necessary when there is no other way of treating serious diseases. They can also be used after an operation for an organ transplant, in order to prevent the body rejecting the new organ. Until recently, immunosuppressive drugs had very serious side effects, which could be fatal. New developments and anti-antibodies offer much safer treatment, and have an encouraging success rate.

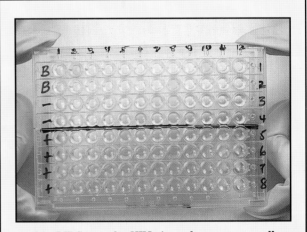

In this AIDS test, the HIV virus shows up as yellow.

AIDS

AIDS (Acquired Immune Deficiency Syndrome) is caused by a virus called the Human Immunodeficiency Virus (HIV for short). The virus is passed from person to person in the blood and in semen during sexual activity. The virus can lie dormant for long periods of time, when the person is infected, but not ill. Eventually, problems start because memory lymphocytes (see page 6) are damaged and the immune system cannot work properly. In time, the entire immune system collapses and the patient soon dies from infection or cancer.

25

LIVING WITH ALLERGIES

Living with an allergy is easier if its cause can be identified and avoided. This may be as simple as avoiding cats if the allergen is cat fur, or as inconvenient as a gluten-free diet for sufferers of celiac disease. Often, the cause of an allergy is not known, and a doctor may treat uncomfortable symptoms with drugs. Patients must follow instructions carefully in order to gain the benefits that drugs can offer and to reduce the damaging side effects that they can cause.

It is in everyone's interest that the environment in which we live should be as healthy as possible. We all need clean air, which is as free from pollution as possible. We all need healthy food. Chemicals and other possible allergens should be handled with extreme caution, and they should be used only when absolutely necessary. There is a great deal that can be done to ensure that the world is a safer place for us all, and for our children and grandchildren after us.

Alternative foods

People who suffer from allergies to foods need to take special care of themselves in the following ways.
* Only eat tiny amounts of suspect foods.
* Take care with foods which are from the same food type as the allergen.
* Always read food labels carefully.
* Be careful about eating in other people's homes and in restaurants. Always warn hosts of a serious food allergy. Children should take their own food to parties and on outings.

Many alternative foods are now available.

Celiac Society

There are a number of self-help groups which give help and support to people with allergies and immune disorders. The Celiac Society helps people with celiac disease by publishing newsletters, diet leaflets and recipes. It is also involved in fundraising in order to support research into the disease. The society arranges meetings locally for sufferers of the disease and their carers. In this way, fellow sufferers can meet and share their experiences. Its address, and the addresses of similar kinds of organizations, are given at the end of this book.

Hypo-allergenic products

People with allergies, especially those with allergies to cosmetics, do not have to go without these things altogether. A wide range of hypo-allergenic skin care and cosmetic products is now available. Hypo-allergenic products contain no perfume or coloring, so are less likely to cause an allergic reaction than normal products. Allergy sufferers can now buy soap, perfume and makeup for only a few cents more than the cost of their normal equivalent. Hypo-allergenic products are recommended for anyone with delicate skin and they are essential for people who suffer from allergies, unless they are willing to do without these things altogether! The products are useful for babies and children who are sensitive to skin preparations, even those that are specially prepared for them.

Hypo-allergenic products make skin care safer.

Infantile eczema

Infantile eczema usually improves during childhood and may disappear altogether. Creams and ointments can help to control the problem. The following steps may also help:
* Avoid putting anything next to the skin which may irritate it, especially wool.
* Use skin moisturizers to keep the skin soft.
* Avoid extremes of hot and cold.
Eczema is not infectious and cannot be caught by coming into contact with it.

Infantile eczema often clears up on its own.

The inheritance of allergies

The tendency for people to suffer from allergies clearly runs in families, although not everyone who has an allergy is closely related to someone else who has one. It is usually only the tendency to suffer that is passed on. In other words, allergies are not passed on in the same way that, for example, eye color is. If both parents have blue eyes it is very likely that their children will have blue eyes. If, however, both parents suffer from hay fever, their children will not necessarily suffer from this type of reaction, but instead may experience different allergic disorders. For example, their children may have asthma or eczema. Children of parents who have allergies will not always have allergies themselves, and it is not usually possible to predict who will be affected.

A few of the rare immune deficiency disorders are inherited directly. Predictably, this is because of specific defects in a family's genetic makeup. These families may need genetic counseling before starting a family.

Living with asthma

Good management of asthma involves the proper use of drugs (see page 22). In addition, it is helpful to maintain clean, dust-free living conditions and to reduce exposure to animals. Plenty of fresh air and exercise will help to maintain good health and fitness. Regular checkups are needed, but the most important people involved in monitoring their condition are the asthmatics themselves and their families. The amount of air which is breathed in and out can now be measured quite simply with an inexpensive peak flow meter (see page 23). This not only monitors the control of air on a regular basis, but also gives advance warning of specific attacks. Some infections, particularly chest infections, can cause asthma attacks and prompt treatment is needed.

Asthmatics can make top athletes.

Allergies at work

Many of the chemicals used in the manufacturing processes in factories can cause allergic reactions. Machine oils, which are used as lubricants in metalworking, are a particular problem, as well as chemicals used in the gasoline, oil-refining, agricultural and plastics industries. Workers can reduce the hazards of an allergic reaction to such chemicals by wearing suitable protective clothing at all times.

Agricultural workers need protection from chemicals.

Preventing AIDS

AIDS is the most serious public health problem today. The virus which causes AIDS is passed in blood and semen in three ways.
* Drug addicts who inject drugs into their veins often share dirty needles with other addicts and are at great risk.
* The virus may be passed during sexual activity.
* The virus was passed in infected blood transfusions and blood products (like plasma) before the risk of AIDS was fully understood by doctors.

As yet there is no prospect of a cure for AIDS, nor any effective immunization against it. Prevention is the only weapon we have.

The prevention of AIDS depends on educating people, particularly those at risk.
* Ideally, drug addicts should stop injecting into their veins. Failing this, they should not use dirty needles. In some countries, addicts are now supplied with free sterile needles.
* Everyone needs to take great care in their sexual relationships, by limiting the number of sexual partners and always using a condom.
* Blood donors are now tested for HIV, and blood products are treated to kill any virus which is present.

Living in a bubble

Our bodies are wonderfully equipped to keep us safe. The skin forms a tough waterproof covering to keep out harm. Any harmful substances which do get through can be recognized and eliminated quickly. The antibodies even remember how to react to a threat in the future. The body's ability to repair itself is truly amazing. A program of renovation and repair goes on all the time. It is only when these systems fail that there is a problem. Fortunately, this is rare, and even when allergies do occur, they are usually mild and respond successfully to medical treatment.

A few people are very severely affected by allergic or immune disorders. Even the best available treatment may not improve their condition. These people sometimes have to be isolated from the rest of the world in a special room or "bubble." The air they breathe is filtered to remove all allergens, bacteria, and viruses. Their food has to be specially prepared and sterilized, and they cannot even touch another person directly, in case germs get onto their skin. These people live what must be a lonely existence, but without these extreme precautions they might die from the least infection.

Research into allergies

Scientists are always trying to find out more about how our bodies work both in health and in disease. Transplant surgery and the HIV virus have provided powerful incentives to examine our immune systems in depth. Like all medical research, the work is painstaking and slow, and as one question is answered, three new ones take its place. In transplant surgery, it is vital to have safe, effective drugs which can "damp down" the immune system enough to prevent the new organ being rejected, yet without harming the patient. Improvements in drugs have contributed greatly to the success of transplant surgery.

The battle to understand and defeat AIDS has led to a greater knowledge of how our immune systems work. So far, one drug – zidovudine – has been shown to slow down the progression of AIDS, but a real cure is still a long way off.

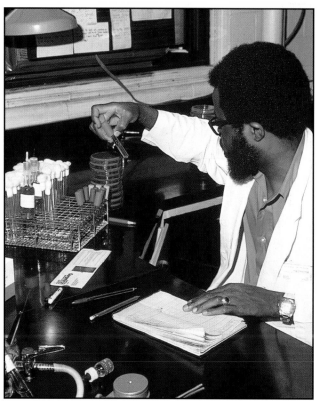

Medical research is painstaking and slow.

Useful addresses

American Allergy Association
P.O.Box 7273
Menlo Park, California 94026
(415) 322-1663
Provides information about allergic free diets coping with various commercial products.

American Celiac Society
45 Clifford Avenue
Jersey City, New Jersey 07304
(201) 432-1207
Non profit corporation formed to provide assistance to persons who are sensitive to glutenate food. Will respond to specific questions from individuals about particular foods.

Asthma and Allergy Foundation of America
1302 18th Street NW
Suite 303
Washington, D.C. 20036
(202) 679-3959
Answers inquiries, provides consulting and reference services.

Center for Hyperactive Children
P.O.Box 406
Murray Hill Station
New York, N.Y.10156
(212) 679-3959
Provides free referral service.

College for Allergy and Immunological Disorders
Baylor College of Medicine
1200 Morsund Avenue
Houston, Texas 77030
(713) 791-4219
Diagnoses and treats persons with allergic and immunological diseases. Answers inquiries, provides counseling services for a fee.

Lupus Network
230 Ranch Drive
Bridgeport, Connecticut 06606
(203) 372-5795
Nonprofit educational organization that provides information to those concerned with lupus.

GLOSSARY

Allergen A harmless substance that enters the body and causes the immune system to react.

Amino acid A chemical substance that makes up proteins.

Anemia The unhealthy condition of not having enough red cells in the blood.

Antibody A specific protein that is produced in the body and that fights against an antigen.

Antigen A potentially harmful substance that causes the body to make an antibody.

Bacteria Microscopic organisms that can cause disease.

Biopsy A sample of tissue that is taken from the body for the diagnosis of a disease.

Bronchus (plural Bronchi) One of the two tubes connecting the windpipe with the lungs.

Cancer A diseased growth in the body.

Cell The smallest unit of living matter.

Diagnosis The identification of a disease or disorder by means of its symptoms.

Heterosexual (activity) Sexual activity between people of the opposite sex.

Histamine An important chemical in the body's allergic response.

Homosexual (activity) Sexual activity between people of the same sex.

Immunization Making people safe against a disease by injecting small doses of the organism which causes the disease.

Immunoglobulin The proteins from which antibodies are made.

Inflammation Swelling and soreness.

Node A swelling or roundish lump.

Nucleus The central part of a cell, which controls its activities.

Organ An essential part of the body with a special purpose, like the heart.

Protein An important chemical in plants and animals which is made up of amino acids.

Semen The male sexual fluid which contains sperm.

Steroid A group of powerful drugs that fight inflammation and are used in a variety of diseases.

Symptom A change in the body or the mind that shows that something is wrong.

Toxin A poisonous substance that is often made by bacteria.

Transplantation Taking an organ from one person's body and placing it in another's.

Virus A tiny, very simple organism that causes infectious disease in the body.

INDEX

AIDS 17, 25, 28, 30
allergens 7, 8, 10, 11, 12, 14, 18-20, 31
allergic response 7
anaphylactic shock 12
animals 10, 23, 28
anti-histamine 12, 19
antibodies 6-8, 13, 15, 16, 18, 31
antigens 6-8, 15, 16, 25, 31
asthma 10-12, 14, 18, 19, 22, 23, 28
atopic eczema 14
atopy 8
auto-immune diseases 8, 16

bacteria 31
biopsy 24, 31
bloodstream 5, 12, 15, 16, 25
blood tests 18, 25
bronchi 11, 22, 31
bronchodilators 22

chemicals 13, 14, 26, 28
celiac disease 8, 13, 24, 26
Celiac Society 26
cosmetics 14, 27
cystic fibrosis 17

desensitization 20
diagnosis 18, 31
drugs 17, 19-23, 25, 26, 28
dust 8, 10, 20, 23

eczema 12, 14, 27

food 13, 14, 17, 18, 24, 26
food additives 13
food allergy 12, 18, 26

gluten 13, 24, 26

hay fever 8, 10, 19-21, 27
histamine 7, 8, 12, 15, 19, 31
hives 12, 19

IgE 6-8, 12
immune cells 4-6, 17, 20
immune complex 6, 8, 13, 19
immune deficiency disorders 17, 27
immune system 4-7, 17, 20, 25
immunoglobulins 6, 7, 16, 17, 31
immunosuppressive drugs 25
infantile eczema 27
infection 4, 5, 12, 17, 25, 28, 29
inflammation 7, 8, 11, 31

leukemia 17
lupus erythematosus 16
lymph nodes 4, 5
lymphatic vessels 4, 5
lymphocytes 5, 6

macrophages 5, 6, 8
mast cells 5, 7, 11, 19
memory lymphocytes 6, 25
molds 8, 10

nucleus 31

peak flow meter 23, 28
pernicious anemia 8, 16
pollen 8-10, 20, 21
pollution 26, 28
pregnancy 15, 25

rashes 18, 20
research 30
rhesus disease 15, 18, 25
rheumatic fever 16
rheumatoid arthritis 8, 16

skin tests 18
spleen 4
spores 8, 10
steroids 19, 22, 31
stings 12, 15, 20
symptoms 8, 10-12, 18-20, 24, 31

tartrazine 13
tests 18, 19, 23-25
thymus 4
transplants 17, 25, 30, 31

villi 13
virus 31

Photographic Credits:
Cover and pages 21 top, 23 top and 28 bottom: Robert Harding Library; pages 5 left and right, 6, 7 left and right, 9 both, 10 bottom, 12 top, 13 bottom, 14 middle, 15 left, 17, 18 bottom, 19, 22 top and bottom, 23 right, 25 left and right and 30: Science Photo Library; pages 8 and 21 bottom: National Pollen and Hay Fever Bureau; page 10 top: Flick Killerby; pages 12 bottom, 14 left and right and 24 top and bottom: Biophoto Associates; pages 13 top, 23 left, 27 bottom and 28: J. Allan Cash Library; page 14 top: National Medical Slide Bank; page 15: Pete Atkinson/Planet Earth; pages 20, 18 top, 26 top and bottom and 27 top: Roger Vlitos; page 25 top: Topham Picture Library; page 29: Frank Spooner Agency.